Stalking

A Handbook for Victims

Emily Spence-Diehl

Learning Publications, Inc.
Holmes Beach, Florida

ISBN 1-55691-161-0

Learning Publications, Inc.
5351 Gulf Drive
P.O. Box 1338
Holmes Beach, FL 34218-1338

Printing: 5 4 3 Year: 4 3 2 1

Printed in the United States of America.

Contents

Illustrations

Introduction

If you're reading this, chances are a stalker has begun to rob you of your sense of control over your life. You may be overwhelmed and unsure of where to turn next. If so, this book is for you. It is written under the guiding belief that *knowledge is power.* By arming you with resources, choices, safety tips and stalker information; I hope you will be able to turn the tide against the stalker and regain some power and control over your life.

The choices are yours . . .

I want to first emphasize the purpose of this book is to present you with *options* not *directions*. It is a *handbook* not an *instruction manual.* There is no "one size fits all" approach to stalking intervention. As you gather information, please know that you must make the choices that work best for you. Trust your gut feelings. If I have discussed an option that you believe won't work for you—*by all means disregard it!* Police officers, counselors, victim advocates, prosecutors, friends, co-workers and family are all part of a team intended to help you — *but you are the team leader.*

Stalking laws across the country are less than a decade old. Most experts recognize that our knowledge of this crime is in its infancy. Our communities and criminal justice systems are still in the process of learning how to effectively respond. As a victim of this crime, you may have already discovered that most communities are not prepared to deal with the ongoing and unpredictable nature of stalking. It is for this reason that it is critical for you to know the full range of your rights and options. Since our knowledge of stalking is growing so rapidly, you may wish to use this book as a supplement to a broader search for information. Explore your own local policies and state laws to discover the extent of protection available to you. If you don't know where to begin, you may find it helpful to start with the toll-free national numbers listed in Appendix E.

Victim or Survivor?

There has been much debate on the use of the words victim and survivor. Some believe that the word victim carries a negative social stigma and that if you have lived through a crime, you are a survivor. While I hope you choose the terminology that is most comfortable for you, I have chosen to primarily use the term "victim" in this book. The reality is that stalking is an ongoing form of *victimization.* If I refer to you as a "victim," I am simply expressing that *something is happening (or has happened) to you against your will.* In no way do I intend it as a reflection of who you are. If anything, as a professional victim advocate and counselor, I have found crime victims to be some of the most strong and courageous among us. I firmly believe that no one chooses or desires to be victimized. Furthermore, there is nothing in the world that someone can do to "make" another person stalk him or her. Stalking originates only in the mind of the perpetrator — not in the behavior or appearance of the victim.

As a final note, I wish to commend you for taking steps to gain back control. You are experiencing one of the very worst crimes against humanity. You may be feeling isolated, misunderstood and terrified — a prisoner in your own home. I sincerely hope that the information you find here will arm you with helpful knowledge and shed light on the path towards healing and safety. Though there are no easy answers, please know that you are not alone. There are 1.4 million Americans stalked annually, and individuals across the country are working tirelessly to provide them support and assistance. Help is out there and together we can wage a war against this insidious crime.

Acknowledgments

I would like to acknowledge the countless survivors of stalking who have shared their pain, trauma, triumphs, tragedies, and successes with me. I can think of no other group more courageous or resilient than these women and men. For those individuals who were specifically interviewed for this book, I wish to specially thank them for their kindness and willingness to help others. By their request, no names have been used to protect their privacy, however, I sure hope they realize the important contributions they have made to this effort.

I also wish to show appreciation for my family, Isabelle Owen Spence, Charles Spence, Brad Spence, Jeff Spence, and Elizabeth Owen, my wonderful husband Greg, and my mentor, Dr. Patricia Telles-Irvin.

1
Know Thy Enemy

This chapter explores the elements of stalking and describes the character traits and tactics used by stalkers. It is entitled "Know Thy Enemy" because it is believed that in order to effectively respond to stalking, one must understand certain characteristics of stalking and its perpetrators. We often initially react to stalkers with the presumption they are "reasonable" individuals. Yet, nothing could be farther from the truth. When you try to reason with a stalker, he or she manipulates that interaction and gains feelings of control through your willingness to negotiate. Once you are able to look through the lens of a stalker (i.e., knowing thy enemy), it is easier to develop your own tactical responses.

> *The more I gave in to his pleas to meet or talk with him, the more power he had over me, even though he made me believe I was the one in control.* **Stalking Survivor**

What is Stalking?

In the most basic terms, stalking is unwanted pursuit, following, or harassment. Legally, many states define stalking as the willful, malicious and repeated following or harassment of another person. To harass means to "engage in a course of conduct directed at a specific person that causes substantial emotional distress in such person and serves no legitimate purpose" (Florida Statute 784.048). The legal language was developed to be flexible enough to include a wide variety of stalking behaviors and rigid enough to prevent misuse of the law. All 50 states have anti-stalking codes, with some variation from state to state. Some states have misdemeanor and felony levels of stalking, while others just have one or the other. A misdemeanor is a lower-level crime typically punishable by less than one year in jail, while felonies can carry prison sentences between one year and life. Often, misdemeanors are perceived as "a slap on the wrist." First offenses are frequently not adjudicated (they won't show up as a criminal record) and carry punishments involving only community service and probation.

In addition, some states require direct threats while others do not. A victim may be experiencing extreme terror and feelings of harassment, but be unable to seek legal assistance due to the lack of an explicit threat of harm. To find out about the specific code in your state, contact your local State Attorney's office (District Attorney) or the National Victim Center (see Appendix E). Keep in mind that your experiences may constitute the *situation of stalking*, but haven't yet escalated to a point that they fall under the legal (criminal) definition. If this is the case, please know that taking personal steps to stop the stalking at the earliest possible point is critical, whether or not your state considers it illegal.

Elements of Stalking

Each stalking behavior by itself may or may not be illegal and generally does not constitute the crime of stalking. When these behaviors are viewed together, however, a pattern emerges that serves no other purpose than to annoy, alarm, or terrorize a victim. Despite the development of stalking laws across the nation, stalking remains an under-detected crime that is hard to prove and terrifying to experience. The following pages describe the various elements of stalking, ranging from the least to the most intrusive (see Figure 1).

Information Gathering

Imagine spending all day, everyday thinking of ways to terrorize an individual. The obsessive nature of stalkers allows them

Figure 1. Frequency and Escalation of Stalking Behaviors

100%

- ✗ Information gathering from friends, post office, internet, employer, school, etc.
- ✗ Repeated non-threatening mail, e-mail, beeper codes, and phone calls.
- ✗ Persistent physical approaches and/or requests for dates, meetings, etc.
- ✗ Notes or flowers left on your car.
- ✗ Observing/following and "coincidentally" showing up wherever the victim goes.
- ✗ Sitting outside your home or place of employment.
- ✗ Waiting next to your car in the parking lot.
- ✗ False reports to authorities, spreading rumors, giving misinformation or secrets to friends/family.

50%

- ✗ Vandalism or destruction of property.
- ✗ Threatening mail, e-mail, notes, phone calls, and/or beeper codes. Threats may be direct, implied, or symbolic.
- ✗ Leaving evidence that car has been broken into.
- ✗ Breaking into the victim's home when he or she is not there.
- ✗ Breaking into the victim's home when he or she is there.
- ✗ Leaving dead animals in home or car.

25%

- ✗ Physically attacking the victim (e.g., grabbing, hitting, pushing, etc.)
- ✗ Rape or attempted rape.

<2%

- ✗ Murder or attempted murder.

Frequency data based on research by Meloy 1996; Tjaden and Thoennes 1998; and Pathé and Mullen 1997.

to do just that. This enormous time commitment to the crime of stalking allows perpetrators to generate exhaustive ways to terrorize and harass their victims.

Many stalkers begin by gathering information about their victims. Former intimate partners certainly have a head start in this area, and often use very personal information to blackmail their victims. Most stalkers, including former intimates, need to gain information about the whereabouts, lifestyles, routines, investments (personal and financial), work environments, and family of their victims.

Potential sources of information that stalkers may tap into and manipulate are:

- Co-workers
- Classmates
- Friends
- Relatives
- Department of Motor Vehicles (vehicle registration and license)
- City utilities (water, sewer, electricity)
- State professional licensing boards
- Voter Registration
- Veterinarians
- The Post Office
- Phone Companies
- Internet search engines (there is even a world wide web site devoted exclusively to helping stalkers access personal information)
- Human resources departments at workplaces
- Banks
- Credit card companies

Despite the confidentiality that many of the above listed sources claim to provide, through clever lying and manipulation stalkers are able to access private information. They may seek information from the victim him or herself or from family, friends, acquaintances, and co-workers. For example, the stalker may pose as a family member with a serious emergency to get the unlisted phone number of a victim from a telephone operator. Additionally, some sources of information may also be used as a tool for harassment. The stalker may file complaints of ethical violations with professional licensing boards, or hit and run complaints with the department of motor vehicles and law enforcement agencies.

> *The most frightening thing was that he would tell me very personal information that no one else would have known. It made me feel paranoid that he was watching me all day.* **Stalking Survivor**

Unwanted Contacts — Gifts, Notes, Calls, Following, and Observation

Unwanted contacts are the most common elements of stalking. Sometimes stalkers initially come across as charming by leaving gifts, flowers, love letters, or poems for their objects of interest (potential victims). When it becomes apparent these gestures do not have their desired effects (i.e., you didn't fall madly in love with the stalker), contacts can turn ugly and frightening. Gifts of dead flowers, hateful letters, or even dead animals may replace the original non-threatening objects of affection.

The telephone is another favorite tool of the stalker. Hang-up calls, answering machine messages, and persistent attempts to engage the victim in conversation are all too common. Though Caller ID may have initially thwarted stalkers, they quickly learned to dodge this roadblock through the call-block functions and the use of payphones. Additionally, victims who use beepers may be subjected to continuous threatening or harassing "beeper codes" left on their paging devices.

Another form of harassment is to "coincidentally" show-up wherever the victim goes — parties, the fitness center, the movies, the grocery store, school, work, and so on. Stalkers may simply stand within an observable distance of the victim, or some may approach and attempt conversation. If the stalker has not been detected by the victim during observation, he or she may call at a later time to inform the victim of the contact, i.e., "That was a nice blue shirt you had on last night."

This type of tracking and following makes it extremely difficult for victims to elude stalkers. Many victims change residences, phone numbers, and daily routines to no avail. The stalkers manipulate new numbers from unsuspecting phone operators, follow the victims home from work, and/or get the new information from acquaintances. For the stalker, it becomes a game of cat and mouse. But for the victim it becomes a nightmare with no predictable endpoint.

Escalation — Vandalism, Threats, and Violence

Some stalkers never escalate beyond unwanted contacts and information gathering. Others, however, continue to worsen over time through increased threats, vandalism, and violence. Since our knowledge of the crime is still in its infancy, it is difficult to predict who may or may not become more violent or threatening. At this time, the most reliable predictor is the stalker's previous behavior— if he or she has a history of violent behavior (especially domestic violence), there is a strong likelihood that the stalker will become violent again. However, under any circumstance victims should be cautious since some stalkers with no previous history of violent behavior have been known to escalate to a more dangerous level. Some states don't identify stalking as a crime until "credible threats" of bodily harm are made. This is unfortunate since key points of early intervention that may prevent further escalation are missed.

Stalkers have learned how to take vandalism to a new level of terror. It is common for stalkers to break into vehicles (leaving no external traces) and either remove parts of the interior, re-arrange mirrors and seat positions, or damage the interior. Stalkers want their victims to know it was not some random act of vandalism, but intentional terrorism instead. As they escalate, similar traces are left in the victims' homes, representing further intrusion into private spaces. Furniture may be rearranged, photographs stolen or relocated, or other clues left to demonstrate the stalkers presence (the bed looks slept-in). These forms of vandalism are especially tricky since a victim may not be taken very seriously by law enforcement officers with a complaint that someone "broke into my car and rearranged my seats and mirrors." In these situations, the victims may be perceived as the ones who are mentally ill, instead of the stalkers.

> *Sometimes I would unlock my car and find a rose on the seat — no note, just the flower. I knew he somehow got into my car and left it there; it was all he needed to do to terrorize me.* **Stalking Survivor**

Threats to the victims (as well as their loved ones) may be explicit and direct or indirectly implied. Explicit threats, such as letters describing potential death or injury, are the easiest to use when bringing legal action against stalkers. Many stalkers recognize this and are more likely to resort to implied or symbolic threats, or direct threats that cannot be traced back to the stalker. A common implied threat is a torn or altered photograph of the victim. Symbolic threats, such as the abduction of a family pet, can be extremely terrorizing for the victim and serve to demonstrate the stalker's control over the victim's life.

Less than one-quarter of stalking cases escalate to the level of physical violence. In these cases, the victim as well as his or her loved ones become potential targets of violent attacks. If the stalker claims romantic interest in the victim, rape or attempted rape may be an additional concern. Few stalkers resort to murder (less than two percent), yet our ability to predict who will be homicidal is limited, leaving many victims to be paralyzed by the fear of this possibility (Meloy 1996). When stalkers resort to any form of violence it is important for victims and their loved ones to take all safety pre-cautions and seek as much outside help as possible. No threat should be dismissed or underestimated.

Stalkers — Traits and Tactics

It has only been recently that researchers, psychologists, and law enforcement have begun to take a closer look at the traits and tactics of the everyday stalkers (as opposed to celebrity and other "high profile" stalkers). The characteristics described in Figure 2 and the next few pages are based on professional observations and academic or forensic (criminal) research. As more and more victims come forward to seek help, we will be able to establish more accurate profiles of various types of stalkers.

Rejection

The perception of rejection is a common denominator among nearly all stalkers. The rejection may be either real or contrived in the mind of the stalker. The victim may not have responded (in the way the stalker hoped) to romantic overtures, a relationship (romantic or friendship) may have ended, an employee (or co-worker) may have been fired, a student might have been given an unsatisfactory grade, a member of a cult or gang might have quit, or the stalker may perceive a "value" rejection (e.g., stalking of abortion clinic doctors).

For stalkers, it is not the manner of the rejection that is important, only the rejection itself. There is no good way to "let down" a stalker. In fact, some stalkers may perceive the marriage or dating of their victim (to another) to be a personal rejection, even when there never existed an intimate relationship between the stalker and victim. Ironically, stalkers perceive themselves as the "true victims." Many believe they have been teased, misled, trampled on, abandoned, abused, and simply wronged. No matter how illogical or untrue are these perceptions, the stalkers cling tightly to them and cannot be reasoned with. In fact, many stalkers move from one "impossible" obsession to the next. The abandonment (rejection)

Figure 2. Common Stalker Characteristics

- Jealous
- Narcissistic
- Obsessive and compulsive
- Falls "instantly" in love
- Manipulative
- Does not take responsibility for own feelings or actions
- Needs to have control over others
- Socially awkward or uncomfortable
- Views self as a victim of society, family, and others
- Unable to take "no" for an answer
- Deceptive
- Often switches between rage and "love"
- Difficulty distinguishing between fantasy and reality
- Sense of entitlement ("You owe me . . . ")
- Unable to cope with rejection
- Dependent on others for sense of "self"
- Views his or her problems as someone else's fault
- May be of above average intelligence

they hate and fear the most becomes a self-fulfilling prophecy resulting from their own erratic and irrational behaviors.

> *It doesn't matter whether you love them, hate them, give them compassion or give them anger . . . they'll take any emotion you offer. Whatever you have, they'll take it. All they really want is a reaction — good or bad. There's nothing you can do to please this person."*
>
> **Stalking Survivor**

Obsession

As the stalking behaviors persist, the daily life of the stalker becomes more and more revolved around that of the victim. It is not uncommon for stalkers to be obsessive about many aspects of their life, such as work and home habits. This trait was well demonstrated in the movie, *Sleeping With The Enemy*, where the controlling and abusive husband insisted that all the soup cans in the cabinet be facing the same way. Stalkers' thought patterns tend to be repetitive in nature and they are unable to refocus on anything except their objects of interest, i.e., their victims.

> *I wish I knew what about me he likes so much — I would either market it or get rid of it.* **Stalking Survivor**

The level of danger increases for the victim when the stalker's obsession grows to the point that he or she ceases to be functional, i.e., eating, sleeping and work become less important than thoughts and actions relating to the victim. When stalkers become willing to allow their job or academic security to suffer, their ability to set priorities is severely impaired. The more dependent the stalker is on the obsession, the more dangerous the situation is for the victim.

> *Nothing else seemed to matter. He had tunnel vision. I was only person he could see in his life.* **Stalking Survivor**

Fantasy

For many stalkers, the line between fantasy and reality is either blurry or non-existent. The fantasy themes often revolve around entitlement ("you're mine"), anger ("you'll pay for this") and/or destiny ("we're meant to be together"). In some cases, the belief that the fantasy is real is so strong that the stalkers may appear more reliable and insistent than the victims. Law enforcement officers may call a stalker in for an interview who very convincingly spins a tale about the love relationship between he or she and the victim, right down to the insignificant details. Yet in reality no romantic relationship ever existed. These particular types of stalkers are referred to by psychological experts as sufferers of "erotomania"; they delusionally believe they're in a romantic relationship with the victim that does not actually exist. These individuals represent a small percentage of all stalkers. The majority of stalkers, however, engage in some degree of fantasy, but maintain a stronger hold on reality. For example, a stalker may truly believe that he or she is *destined* to be romantically linked with the victim, but understands that he or she is not currently in a romantic relationship with that individual (i.e., "Someday we'll be together.").

Narcissism

While many think narcissism is simply a love of oneself, with stalkers it is more often observed as an inability to recognize or respect the needs and feelings of others. Stalkers believe their own thoughts and actions take priority over all others. This is especially true in situations where there was a previous intimate relationship between the stalker and the victim. The stalker will justify his or her behavior with the belief that "If I'm suffering, so should you." Because they lack the appropriate coping skills, they are unable to tolerate discomfort, rejection, loss, shame, or embarrassment. Furthermore, they are either unaware of or not concerned with the discomfort and pain they may be causing others. The statement, "If I can't have you, no one can," is the ultimate representation of a narcissistic belief of ownership.

Psychological Profiles

Scientific research that profiles stalkers is just now beginning to flourish. Some researchers have studied celebrity stalkers, while others have focused their attention on those who have been incarcerated. Unfortunately, these populations are not representative of all the stalkers in the country. Celebrity stalkers and those who have been convicted and jailed are a small minority in a population of perpetrators who are able to skirt the law and terrorize everyday people. Categories of stalkers have been established around such differences as the following:

- The level (degree) of stalkers' beliefs (erotomania and borderline erotomania) (Meloy 1989).
- The type of relationship (if any) that existed prior to the stalking (intimate relationship, acquaintance, casual date, employment related, stranger).
- Whether the goal of the stalker is to attach (have a relationship), be vindicated ("be right") or get revenge ("punish") (Lindsey 1993).
- Whether they are anti-social or functioning in a social environment (still working, eating, grooming, etc.) (Lindsey 1993).

However the divisions are made, experts generally agree that all stalkers are diagnosable with one or more mental disorders. Most victims, though, don't need science to tell them that their stalkers are mentally ill. Furthermore, research of incarcerated stalkers has shown them to be of much higher intelligence than other criminals, socially isolated, having histories of failed interpersonal relationships, and lacking in social skills (Meloy 1996). Through preliminary research, it is clear that there is not a single "stalker profile." The best method to categorize (profile) stalkers, however, is yet to be agreed upon in the scientific and criminal justice communities.

Manipulation

What the stalker lacks in social skills is more than made up for in the ability to manipulate people. In order to serve their narcissistic needs, stalkers enlist others to help gather information about their victims. Stalkers manipulate their victims in some of the following ways to establish contact and feed their obsessions:

- ***Uses guilt:*** guilt trips are stalkers' favorite tools. "I have something really important to talk to you about, but it's too hard to do it over the phone." "You're the only one who really understands me, I can't talk to anyone else about this." "Why are you doing this to me? Don't you care about me?"
- ***Promises "one last time":*** the stalker dangles the carrot of "closure" to draw the victim in. "I'll never bother you again."
- ***Uses blackmail:*** whether or not you've ever done anything slightly improper, stalkers will either find or fabricate something to blackmail you with. Sometimes the items they use to blackmail were initiated by them in the first place, leaving us to wonder if it was all part of the plan. "I'll send those nude photo's from our vacation to the newspaper." "I'll tell your boss about the time you called in sick." "I'll tell everyone you're a whore." "I'll file a report of child abuse against you."
- ***Unfounded accusations:*** stalkers often know what you might be sensitive about and intentionally find your most vulnerable "buttons" to press. "I knew you were a bitch like all the others." "You think you're better than everyone else." "You don't care about anyone but yourself."
- ***Twists words:*** the stalker turns the victim's words around to meet his or her own needs. "You're just saying that you don't want to see me to keep your family off your back." "I know that you really do love me and that your friends are just trying to brainwash you against me."
- ***Gives gifts:*** the stalker may give expensive or time-intensive gifts to the victim to facilitate a response. Dozens of roses, elaborate poems, or extremely generous gestures (paying for a car repair), all might be used as emotional

"ammunition" at a later date. "After all I've done for you."

Not only do stalkers often succeed in manipulating their victims; anyone associated with the victim can be targeted as well. A well-meaning parent might be manipulated into giving the stalker the victim's address because the stalker claimed to be planning a class reunion. Stalkers learn to become masters of deception.

Gender

Both men and women are known to be stalkers. There are more male than female stalkers and more female than male victims — but both genders are well represented on either side of the crime. One should never assume that a female stalker wouldn't resort to violence purely on the basis of gender. Women represent a growing number of violent offenders in many types of crimes. They can be violent toward men and other women. In fact, a common type of female-female stalking is that of one woman stalking the current love interest of her ex-partner. Additionally, men's claims of being stalked by women should be taken just as seriously as those cases where the gender breakdown is reversed. Too often, it is assumed that men can "take care of themselves," and their cases are not appropriately addressed until they have escalated out of control. A recent study indicated that the levels of violence against male and female stalking victims were the same (Spitzberg, Nicastro, and Cousins 1998).

2

Taking Action: Practical and Legal Options

Many stalking victims have early misgivings about the stalker prior to the onset of intrusive and invasive behaviors. This is by far the best time to address the problem. Early intervention is the most potent tool a victim can use to address the festering obsession of the stalker. Unfortunately, some victims are ill-advised to take a "wait-and-see" approach to the problem. Waiting for the stalker's obsession to intensify will often force victims to resort to more aggressive and drastic measures later on.

Pre-Stalking: The First Warning Signals

It is recommended that at the first sign of discomfort, the victim clearly communicate an unwillingness to engage in further contact with the stalker. Many victims fear taking an early firm stance and pose the question, "What if he or she isn't really a stalker?". In these situations, it is important to acknowledge those gut feelings that are causing you to worry in the first place. Too often, we worry about hurting peoples' feelings (even potential stalkers with whom we have no desire to have a relationship). Consider that in the long run, it might be better to risk hurting someone's feelings now, than be terrorized by that person in the future.

Also, keep in mind that being compassionate *and* self-protective are not mutually exclusive. You are not obligated to continue or establish an unhealthy (or potentially unhealthy) relationship with anyone, be it friendly or romantic. **Setting firm personal boundaries based on another's erratic or obsessive behavior is not rude.** The stalker might label it as rude or cruel, but this is usually done to manipulate you or make you feel guilty. To try and cease all contact, simply state what you've observed ("you called me six times last night and showed up at my office twice this week"), and tell the stalker that because of your discomfort with these behaviors you'd prefer not to carry on any type of a relationship. If you do this in a non-accusational manner (i.e., focus on your own feelings of discomfort) you can feel secure that no matter what the stalker says or does, you've done nothing cruel or inappropriate.

Communicating With the Stalker: Issuing The No-Contact Statement

Though early intervention is effective in many situations, there are some stalkers who are not dissuaded by a victim's established boundaries. For legal support in the future, there must be evidence that the victim has directly instructed the stalker to stay away. It is important that the stalker hear (or read) on *one* occasion that you do not want any type of contact with him or her (see Figure 3). *It is critical* that this only happens *once!* Any form of communication after the initial "no-contact" statement will be considered by the stalker as a reason to hope and persist. If you break your no-contact statement even one time, the stalker will assume that you may break it again, and he or she will continue.

> *I wish I'd stuck to my guns and not let him manipulate me into talking to him. It was always, "Please, I promise this is the last time." But it never was . . .*
>
> **Stalking Survivor**

Again, whether in person, in writing, through e-mail or on the phone, it is best not to communicate *at all* with the stalker. It is

Figure 3
Sample No-Contact Statements

- *I'm not interested in having a relationship with you. Do not continue to call, stop by, or have any contact with me whatsoever.*
- *I want you to stop trying to contact me. If I discover that you have followed me, been on my property, or called my work or home, I will call the police and file stalking charges.*
- *I am ending our relationship. Do not make any attempt to try and renew it. I will not change my mind. I do not wish to have any contact with you now or in the future. If you try to contact me, I will take legal action against you.*
- *I will no longer tolerate this harassment. If you try to contact me in any shape or form, I will call the police.*

often hard to cease communication with a stalker with whom you have had a previous relationship. These stalkers may know intimate secrets and will find the most sensitive "buttons" to push. They may make threats, blackmail you, use guilt, or manipulate your family and/or children. It is important, even in these difficult situations, to maintain a consistent "no communication" stance. If information must be passed to the stalker (i.e., custody arrangements), do so only through a third party.

> *It's basically a question of survival of the fittest. You have to stay in control — the second you lose control, he has a window of opportunity and knows he can get you.*
> **Stalking Survivor**

The Criminal and Civil Justice Systems: Building a Case

Whether or not you wish to file formal charges against the stalker (or are legally able to do so), it is important to think in terms of building a prosecutable case from the very beginning. You may believe that evidence gathering should be the concern of law enforcement officers and state attorneys, yet in the crime of stalking, victims are often the only ones doing the initial work. This may be due to the relative newness of stalking laws as well as the inherent difficulty in "proving" that the crime is occurring.

> *He's done a million things to me, and I just don't respond. I know that eventually he's going to do something to incriminate himself.* **Stalking Survivor**

It is an unfortunate heavy burden, but you as the victim must approach each stalking behavior with the following questions:

- Were there any witnesses who will support me?
- Is there any evidence that I can physically keep?
- If this happens again, is there any way that I can gather evidence next time?
- Should I call law enforcement right now to report it?

It is helpful to early on locate a victim advocate in your area to assist you. If you are unsure of how to find an advocate, please refer to the resources in Appendix E. The sad truth is that many stalking victims aren't taken seriously until the case has escalated to a frightening level. Because of this problem, it is so important for victims to seek help from as many people as possible, and to assertively advocate on your own behalf. You might have to be very persistent.

Start from the Beginning: Just the Facts

In order to start building a prosecutable case that will be taken seriously by law enforcement, it is critical to write down everything that has happened in chronological order in a journal. Do your best to remember dates and details. This will become your master list that you will continue to add to as new stalking behaviors occur. Keep in mind the "stick to the facts" principle when creating this list. If you decide to report the case to the police, they will need to know specific details, such as "On September 14, around 3:00 p.m., Joe Stalker drove down my street and parked his car directly across from my house. He stayed there, staring at my house, until 9:00 p.m. that evening. I did not leave my house at all during that time. My neighbor, Ms. Brown, stated to me the next day that she observed him doing this as well." For a Sample Stalking Journal, see Appendix A.

Other useful tips to assist the development of a prosecutable case are as follows:

- ✓ If you have filed more than one police report, ask the department to file them together, or make reference in each one to the previous reports. This is especially important in large police departments that maintain a variety of separate units.
- ✓ If you have filed police reports in separate jurisdictions, make sure that each jurisdiction has copies of the others' reports. It is imperative that all reports be viewed together as a "pattern of behavior."

- ✓ If you are awaiting an outcome from a particular officer or detective, feel free to initiate calls yourself and check for updates. Detectives and officers often carry enormous caseloads and work varying hours. You are helping them if you save them the effort of trying to track you down.
- ✓ If you can bring a victim advocate (who you believe will be respected by the officers), do so when you are filing a report. The presence of a third party seems to have a beneficial effect on the filing process.
- ✓ Get a copy of your state's stalking law before you ever try to file a report. Frequently, stalkers are charged with the crime of the moment (aggravated assault, burglary, etc.), rather than the crime of stalking which is based upon a cumulation of events. If the officer has not mentioned stalking, bring it up and ask if he/she believes it is possible to charge the perpetrator with that crime as well.
- ✓ Report each incident, no matter how insignificant it may seem. Law enforcement can write "incident reports," rather than filing charges, and these can later help support the overall stalking case (demonstrating a pattern of behavior).
- ✓ Keep all evidence. No matter how disgusting or offensive, do not throw anything away. Give it to the police. Keep letters, flowers, gifts, and anything else that can be physically collected. It is not necessary for you to read every letter, you can instead give them directly to a police officer or victim advocate to read and keep for you.
- ✓ If you are an Internet user and are receiving harassing e-mail messages, contact (or have the police contact) the server from which the harassing mail is coming from. The double-edged sword of threatening e-mail messages is that everything is traceable, even many files that have already been deleted. Many police departments now have computer specialists who specifically track criminals on the Internet.

- ✓ Do not change your phone number. Instead, install a new unlisted line and keep the old line connected to an answering machine that uses removable cassettes. Give the new number only to those whom you trust the most. If the stalker leaves messages on your machine, remove the cassette, date it, and keep it as evidence.
- ✓ Tell everyone you are surrounded by on a day-to-day basis that you are being stalked. Describe the stalker and ask them to tell you immediately if they ever see him or her in the vicinity. Stalkers rely on secrecy. *Break the silence and know that you have nothing to be ashamed of; you are the victim, not the criminal.* Also, eyewitness reports are critical in breaking down the "he said, she said" dilemma of prosecution.
- ✓ If you can afford to do so, purchasing or renting a surveillance camera is an excellent way to "stalk the stalker."

Restraining Orders (Injunctions for Protection)

The decision to get a restraining order can be very complex for victims of stalking. Some professionals recommend them wholeheartedly, while others are convinced they are totally useless. When trying to decide whether or not to get a restraining order, the most important thing to recognize is that they provide *absolutely no protection from harm.* They are pieces of paper. By themselves, they do little to stop stalking. In a minority of cases (20 to 30 percent), the stalkers have enough fear of the criminal justice system to stop their harassment of the victims. Though these statistics are rather grim, it is important to recognize the role that restraining orders can play in the criminal justice system.

When a victim has a restraining order, police are often able to make arrests under circumstances in which they previously wouldn't have been able. In some states, a lower level (misdemeanor) crime becomes a serious offense (felony) if a protective order was in place. The key to a restraining order's effectiveness is the willingness of the victim to follow through with reports of violations of that order. In many jurisdictions, a single violation can mean several hours spent in the county courthouse waiting for a judicial hearing. After one or more of these violation hearings, however, the presiding judge may sentence the stalker to several months in jail, allowing the victim a temporary reprieve. Clearly, the restraining order is a tool for the criminal justice system.

Some victims are concerned that the restraining order might trigger a more violent or serious threat from the stalker. This is a valid concern, considering the fact that the stalker's behavior has been brought to the attention of judicial personnel (he or she might claim to feel "humiliated"). For this reason, many victims are quite hesitant to pursue this option. Under these circumstances, victims should weigh the pros and cons of their decision. Perhaps increasing safety protocols while seeking an order for protection might outweigh the risks involved. Realistically, restraining orders can simultaneously increase risk and increase criminal justice protection. Ultimately, the choice is yours. Expecting that a restraining order will be violated, you might wish to consider contacting victim advocates and judicial personnel in your community to investigate how seriously these violations are treated.

Victims' Rights

Many states have adopted laws that protect the rights of victims. These laws might allow victims to be notified of upcoming hearings, provide victim impact statements to the court, and receive financial compensation for lost wages, medical bills, and mental health expenses. Unfortunately, stalking victims are often excluded from financial compensation when there have been no criminal charges relating to physical injury. Until our criminal justice system understands the trauma of stalking, victims will continue to fall through the cracks. Under these circumstances, it would be helpful for victims to apply anyway (risking denial of assistance), so that the need for changes in the system guidelines will be made evident.

As many victims know, the protection given to criminals in our justice system is extensive. "Innocent until proven guilty," a concept established when new American pioneers feared government corruption, has allowed many citizens to escape invalid charges. This protection, however, was not developed during a time where rampant interpersonal violence and victimization was as prevalent or obvious as it is today. Men were allowed to beat their wives with a stick no bigger than a thumb (the rule of thumb), and date rape was two centuries away from becoming a common phrase. Nowadays, victims play a critical role in our justice system. There are efforts underway to establish a victims' rights constitutional amendment, making the rights of victims equally important to the rights of defendants. Until this is passed, victims' rights will vary from state to state. Even when laws are in place, you might be forced to advocate for yourself to obtain the services and rights to which you are entitled. The Attorney General's office in your state should be able to provide you with information regarding your rights and role in the criminal justice system.

3
Safety Planning

There are no easy answers to ensure safety, only helpful tips. Safety in the home, workplace, and areas of frequent travel should all be considered. It is also important to develop safety plans for loved ones, as well as yourself.

Safety in the Home

The first step is to call your local law enforcement agency (police) to conduct a safety review in your home and surrounding areas. These are free services generally available in every community. When possible, follow the recommendations of the officer(s). These changes may be simple or expensive and complex. If it appears as though it will be very costly to make the changes, you may want to ask a victim advocate to check into any available funding sources in your community, including formal "victim services" funds, as well as churches, the Junior League, and other local organizations. It may feel very uncomfortable to ask for financial assistance, but keep in mind that you have not chosen to be a victim. Any way that the community can reduce the vast personal and financial costs of this crime can be helpful in lowering the overall trauma and disruption of your life. If possible, explore the use of the following home safety enhancements:

- ✓ Alarm systems that when set off will immediately notify law enforcement.

- ✓ Pins placed in holes that have been drilled through windows and sliding glass doors (these act as second locks).
- ✓ Motion-detector lights on all sides of the home as well as motion-detector alarms on the inside.
- ✓ Bushes and trees that are trimmed so that it is difficult for a human to hide behind them.
- ✓ Install several different types of locks on entry and bedroom doors, each installed with long screws to make it difficult for them to be kicked in.
- ✓ Panoramic peep holes in each door.
- ✓ Bars that lock across the center of sliding glass doors.
- ✓ A cellular phone that can be used if the outside phone lines are disabled.
- ✓ Notify your neighbors. Instruct them to call you (or the police) if they see or hear anything suspicious.
- ✓ Plan all possible escape routes from your home or apartment.
- ✓ Remove critical documents from your home and place them in a lock box at the bank (birth certificates, social security cards, marriage license, medical prescriptions, etc.).
- ✓ Keep an "escape bag" at a friend's house or other secure location. Fill it with cash, clothing, prescriptions, and copies of important documents. Consider making two bags and leaving one with a trusted friend. If you have to leave quickly, you will not be forced to waste time gathering your belongings.

Finally, you may want to consider a dog only if you are willing to give the attention and love it needs to thrive. When treated well, dogs can provide excellent companionship, warning, and protection. An alert dog can allow you some time to let your guard down and relax.

Safety in the Car

It is helpful to peer inside and underneath your car prior to approaching it closely or getting inside. Tinted windows are dangerous because they may conceal the stalker hiding inside the vehicle. You may believe they will conceal you as you are driving, but most stalkers quickly learn your license plate number. Car alarms may be useful in that many can warn you if the alarm has been set off while you were away. Unfortunately, car alarms are often oversensitive (going off when a truck passes by) or under-sensitive (you can gently get into the trunk without ever setting it off). Below are other important options to consider:

- ✓ When you are driving to and from places of frequent travel (work, school, fitness center, etc.), you may want to learn a variety of different routes. Stalkers rely on predictability, so make it as difficult as you can for them to follow or track your whereabouts.
- ✓ Always drive with all of your car doors locked, from the moment you get inside your vehicle.
- ✓ Leave enough space between yourself and the car in front of you to be able to quickly change lanes when necessary.
- ✓ If you somehow find yourself in the car with the stalker, avoid driving anywhere at all. The more remote the location you are in, the more dangerous it becomes. In such circumstances, do your best to follow your instincts and remain visible to others.
- ✓ Consult with a locksmith about the methods that can be used to break into your car. Inquire about any additional devices that may make it more difficult. Some cars need only a "slim Jim" (long skinny piece of metal) to unlock the door.

Safety at Work

The workplace is often the easiest way for stalkers to contact or observe their victims. For this reason, it is important for employers and co-workers to be made fully aware of the situation. Tell them that under no circumstances should they give any information about you to the stalker. They should also be asked to warn you if they ever see the stalker in the area. The stalker should not be allowed access to you at all. If the stalker is spotted in the vicinity, your employer can call the police to have a trespass warning issued.

You may also want to consider the following:

- ✓ Can you vary your schedule?
- ✓ Can you relocate to another office or site?
- ✓ If your voicemail is recorded with your own voice, can you have someone else record it for you? (Obsessional stalkers often call repeatedly just to hear their victims' voices.)
- ✓ Do you have secured parking? How far do you walk to your workplace? Is there anyone willing to walk you to and from your car?
- ✓ Are there any times you are left alone in your workplace? Can you eliminate these times or do anything to increase your safety while alone?
- ✓ Who at your workplace knows personal information about you, such as your address, social security number, benefits information, and home phone? Have these individuals been warned about your circumstances?

Many people are very under-educated about the crime of stalking. You may find that your employer and co-workers need some quick lessons about what they should and should not do. Sometimes it is helpful to enlist the assistance of a victim advocate who may be able to talk to your co-workers and provide them with informational pamphlets. Make sure they are aware that the stalker will lie and is capable of extreme manipulation. Stalkers are experts at making their victims look like they are the ones with the real problems. Your co-workers need to be prepared to expect this and taught how to respond. Some helpful rules for co-workers, employers, friends, and family are:

- ✓ *Never* give out any information about the victim to the stalker (or anyone else that the stalker may have enlisted to help him or her). No matter how urgent the story sounds don't give in.
- ✓ Do not discuss the victim with the stalker. Avoid using the victim's name and re-direct any communication about the victim. Consider adopting a standard phrase that can be repeated, such as "I am not going to discuss this with you."
- ✓ Stay firm, calm, cool, and collected. Any expression of emotion is a signal to the stalker that he or she may have found a weak point, which will be interpreted as a sign to continue to persist.
- ✓ If you make a threat, follow through with it. Do not say that you are going to call the police and then not do it. Let the stalker know that you are serious.

Safety in Public

Varying your routine and telling only a few people about your plans are two ways to avert the stalker in public. Many victims begin to feel as though their freedom has been robbed from them. The stalker may show up everywhere you go, even when you've been very secretive about your plans. In these circumstances, you may wish to consider some of the following actions:

- ✓ If you have a restraining order (injunction for protection), carry your copy with you everywhere. If you see the stalker, call the police (or quietly ask someone to do so for you so that the stalker doesn't leave before they show-up) and show them your order of protection.
- ✓ Tell your companion(s) and/or host(s) that you are being stalked and ask them to be on the look-out.

- ✓ If you see the stalker, stay calm and *do not talk to him or her.* Any time he or she spends looking at you or talking to you will feed the obsession further. Try to stay outside of the stalkers vision. If possible, seek the assistance of others and consider calling the police.
- ✓ Whatever you do, make sure that you do not find yourself alone anywhere that the stalker can approach you. Do not walk to your car alone. Do not go to the restroom alone. It may be difficult and awkward, but asking a stranger to assist you is better than being surprised by the stalker when you are in a vulnerable position or location.

Identifying Sources of Information

It is helpful to consider all of the ways that the stalker may be able to gather personal information, then take action to reduce the likelihood of this occurring. Some possible options are listed below:

- ✓ ***Phone company:*** call or stop by the phone company and ask to speak with a supervisor. Tell him or her about your situation and ask how they can assist you. Most phone companies have policies and special options to deal with telephone harassment and privacy concerns, such as call tracing and blocking.
- ✓ ***Utilities*** (electric, water, sewer): If these services are registered in your name, ask the company supervisor to provide you with privacy options. Even if they already have a policy to not give out customer information, ask them to specifically mark your file confidential. Sometimes companies can erase your address and phone from the computer screen and place a message on the screen that the information is confidential and is kept in a file.
- ✓ ***Home ownership:*** If you are a homeowner, your name, address and telephone number are often available to the public. Again in this case, call a supervisor at the city hall,

explain your situation, and ask for their assistance to assure your privacy.

- ✓ ***The Post Office:*** If the stalker does not yet know the location of your home, consider using a post office box to receive mail. If you have had to relocate because of the stalker, always use a post office box instead of your home address.
- ✓ ***Internet:*** the Internet is a vast source for an incredible amount of personal information. If you are not a skilled user of the Internet, seek the assistance of someone who is familiar with the various types of personal searches that can be conducted. Most public libraries now have computer terminals with Internet access and librarians who are knowledgeable. Once you (or your computer-literate helper) have identified all or most of the search engines on the Internet, contact (e-mail) each one of them separately to request that your personal information be deleted from their files. This process is very time consuming and requires a lot of checking and re-checking to make sure that the information has been deleted. Additionally, if you have your own e-mail account, contact the webmaster of your server to request that your personal information be kept confidential. Some servers keep "profile" information on their users that is accessible by anyone. If you have voluntarily placed personal information in your profile (such as on America On Line's Member Profiles), it is advisable to remove it. You may also want to consider changing your e-mail address, especially if your current username is your actual first or last name.
- ✓ ***Other sources:*** Stop for a moment and brainstorm who may have personal information about you. The pizza delivery service? Cable company? Health care organization? Church? Fitness Center? School? Video rental store? Drycleaners? Bank? Pharmacy? Local, state, or national organizations (professional or personal). Insurance agency? Landlord? Magazine subscription company?

Credit card companies? Charities? Once you have compiled a list of possible information sources, you may want to contact each one to request their assistance to keep your information private. Some may already have a policy to do so (such as medical professionals), but ask them to consider what they would do if contacted by an individual posing as yourself or a spouse. This person (stalker or stalker's helper) may have your social security number, driver's license number, mother's maiden name, or any other piece of information that companies use to verify an individuals identity. In the most serious cases of stalking, it is critical that each and every possible source of information be notified, and warning codes entered directly into the computer databases. You may need to supply these companies with police reports or enlist the assistance of victim advocates who can request help on your behalf.

Relocation

If the stalking has escalated to a level where you feel you must re-locate to ensure your own safety, the choices that you make during relocation are critical. It is painful enough to give up your residence because of another's threatening behavior. But to do so, and then soon be "found" by the stalker is even more heartbreaking and terrorizing. Prior to moving, generate a list (starting with the sources mentioned above) of all possible sources of information. Carefully choose the ones with whom you will give your new location and phone number. Then, consider the following options:

- ✓ Purchase a post-office box, but preferably not at the location closest to your new residence.
- ✓ Consider using your middle name or a different version of your name when signing up for any services.

- ✓ Any time that you give your name, address and/or phone number to anyone, make sure you tell them you are fleeing a stalker and need to be assured privacy.
- ✓ Don't use credit cards or debit cards to make any purchases. It is too easy to track your whereabouts through credit card traces.
- ✓ If you have moved into an apartment complex, do not put your name on your mailbox.
- ✓ If you have the option, apartments or condominiums on the first floors are the *least* safe choice. The higher the floor, the more difficult it is for burglars to enter through the windows.
- ✓ Consider trading in your car for a different one and obtaining a new license plate number.
- ✓ Consider a residence with 24-hour security available. As soon as you move in, give the security supervisor a description or photograph of the stalker and his or her vehicle.
- ✓ Be very selective about who you give your new address and phone number. In the most extreme circumstances, you may wish to tell only those who know everything that has happened, and who you totally trust.
- ✓ Contact friends and family from locations other than your new home. Discarded phone bills can be obtained from roadside trashcans.

Obviously, the choice to re-locate is one made in the most desperate and difficult of circumstances. The trauma of being pursued makes it extremely difficult to make any decisions, much less a major one such as choosing to move. It is very important to seek assistance in this endeavor. Both emotional and practical support is necessary. You are not expected to be able to think of everything, and in this type of crisis it is simply not possible. Prior to making any decisions, you are encouraged to seek the help and advice of law enforcement professionals, victim advocates, state attorneys, and therapists. In the end, however, trust your own gut feelings. Sometimes professionals provide wonderful and practical advice, and other times they do not fully understand the circumstances, minimize the danger, or have placed an overabundance of faith in our criminal justice system. Keep in mind that your safety is the top priority. If your instincts tell you that you are in danger, follow them.

4

Keeping Your Quality of Life: Self-Care

Each stalking behavior by itself may not seem like such a big deal. But day after day, the unexpected and the unprovoked begin to eat away at your sense of control, well being and security. Stalking victims are perhaps one of the most ignored and minimized populations of crime victims today. As a society, we tend to look at each separate behavior and don't stop to consider the effects of the whole series. The stalker called three times last night, he or she came by your office yesterday, or you saw him/her at the movies last weekend. By themselves, none of these would cause much trauma. But when you are being stalked, each of these behaviors will trigger a biological and psychological fear response. The accumulation of these responses is damaging both physically and emotionally. Recognizing these effects is the first step towards healing and recapturing your sense of self.

> *I was afraid to tell anyone. I thought, "Who would believe me?" It's not easy to describe the fear you have when you see the stalker everywhere you go. I thought people might think I was crazy . . . or making it all up.*
>
> **Stalking Survivor**

Physical Impact

To begin, let's look at the physical effects of stalking. When a person is surprised and/or frightened, he or she may experience a pounding heartbeat, sweaty hands, and an increase in body heat. What many are not aware of, however, are the immediate changes in the body's balance of biochemicals. When a person is under constant or continuous threat of harm, these chemical changes become extremely problematic. Preliminary research has shown that on-going stress or trauma can cause memory problems, exhaustion, short-attention span, and a tendency to verbally recall the trauma in a fragmented fashion. What this means for victims of stalking is that without help, the longer the stalking continues, the more serious the physical effects. Too often, victims witness their lives deteriorate in a domino effect — it becomes hard to concentrate at work or school, remember simple tasks, and have enough energy for family, romantic, and friend relationships. Not only does it disrupt a victim's personal life, but when he or she tries to explain the situation to police or other professional helpers, the story can come out sounding scattered and disjointed. This unfortunately can cause the victim to be perceived more critically or suspiciously than the stalker.

> *You need to be aware all of the time — and that's where the trauma comes in. You're body just can't be alert all of the time.* **Stalking Survivor**

Though these physical effects can be terrible, they do not occur to all victims and can be reduced with a few key actions. First, it is important for victims to become aware of the effects of stress on their bodies. Locate the feelings of physical tension, observe how you feel after a "scare" or contact with the stalker, and monitor your energy, soreness, and tiredness. Exercise is generally considered to be extremely helpful after traumatic experiences. Sweating helps to flush out the stress-related chemicals in the body, while an increased heart rate and muscle exertion helps to release tension. Many victims, however, stop exercising because they no longer feel safe jogging outside or going to the gym. In these circumstances, it may be helpful to explore other options such as purchasing home-use exercise equipment or aerobic videotapes. Whatever you choose, try to not allow the stalker to take away this key method of stress reduction.

While exercise is very important, one must also seek the other end of the spectrum: relaxation. Unfortunately, there is no single relaxation technique that works for everyone in every situation. It is helpful to experiment for a while until you find something that meets your needs. However, like exercise, no one learns to relax during a first attempt. Just as you cannot run a 10-mile race without regular practice, it is impossible to slow your heart rate down, relax your muscles, and feel calm without "working" at it. Daily efforts at relaxation are critical to finding long-term inner peace. You may wish to consider trying any of the following methods of relaxation:

✓ ***Biofeedback:*** This is one of the most structured ways to train your body to relax. Many psychologists and therapists are trained to offer biofeedback sessions. A typical biofeedback protocol would be eight to 12 sessions where your body is hooked up to a computer that is monitoring your heart rate, sweat response, muscle tension, and body temperature. Over the course of several weeks, you are trained to directly regulate these bodily functions using your mind. While many may see this as an impossible task, biofeedback has been scientifically shown to be effective for large groups of people. With regular practice, the positive effects of biofeedback can last a lifetime.

✓ ***Guided visualization:*** At nearly every bookstore, you can find a variety of "relaxation" tapes. While some just have soothing background sounds or music, others use a person's voice to "guide" you to relaxation with suggestions and images. For those who are able to conjure up images in their minds, the guided tapes often work quite well. If you find them to be effective, try to eventually learn to guide yourself into a state of relaxation using the same types of words and suggestions that are on the tape. This is especially important when you have recently been frightened and need a "quick fix" until you get home.

- ✓ ***Massage therapy:*** For many, a professional massage is considered a luxury. For stalking victims, however, massage should be considered therapy. Many of us hold stress and tension in our shoulders, necks, and backs, which regular massage can help to alleviate. Depending on your financial ability, a weekly or monthly massage can greatly help to reduce the physical effects of trauma and stress. If there is a massage school in the area where you live, you might be able to pay less by allowing a student to work on you.
- ✓ ***Environmental change*:** Since many stalking victims reduce the amount of time they spend outside the home, it may help to make purposeful "decorative" changes around the home to promote relaxation. Hot baths, aromatic candles, plants, and soft music have a calming effect on many people. The process of attending to these small details, solely for the purpose of self-care, can be empowering as well.

Though some of these suggestions may sound simple or trite, keep in mind that the cumulative effects of several types of self-care can have a stronger impact than each one by itself.

Psychological Impact

There are so many phases you go through; anger, hurt, denial, being withdrawn and depressed, paranoid, second-guessing yourself, and then all the way back to anger again. **Stalking Survivor**

The mental health impact of stalking is intense and often long lasting. The repeated attacks on one's sense of safety and security are enough for anyone to become overwhelmed. It is critical, however, to recognize that you are not going crazy — you're having normal reactions to an abnormal situation. The experience of stalking changes the ways that you think, feel, and behave towards yourself and others. Recognizing these changes is the first step you can take in learning to control them.

I should have known better . . .

The first thing I had to do was acknowledge that it wasn't my fault. **Stalking Survivor**

Probably the most insidious of all potential effects of stalking is self-blame. This is especially true for those who had previously dated the stalker and are now kicking themselves for their choice of romantic partner. Too often victims begin to believe they must have poor judgement skills. For anyone who experiences self-blame, please know that stalkers do not introduce themselves as potential perpetrators. They don't have "stalker" tattooed on their foreheads — and more importantly, you don't have "victim" tattooed on yours.

It has taken me a long time to realize that I did not ask for him to torment me. . . . It was all his doing.

Stalking Survivor

Only now are experts starting to learn enough about stalkers to identify early "red flag" behaviors. Even with this knowledge, the manipulative nature of stalkers makes it difficult to assess their sincerity and true stability. They are masters of deception and often move from one victim to the next. *They didn't choose you because of who you are, but because of who they are.* Remember this! It's not about how you looked, acted, talked, or carried yourself — it's about the stalker's own deep-seated insecurities and psychological problems.

I'm constantly looking over my shoulder . . .

Though you and your loved ones may label it as "paranoia," keep in mind that fear is an instinctual human function intended to help keep us safe. It is generated from a part of the brain over which we have little or no control. Some level of fear and cautiousness is healthy. When it begins to create serious dysfunction in your life, there is cause for concern. Only you, however, can determine what a reasonable level of fear is for your particular situation. Common examples of fear include the sense that you are constantly looking over your shoulder, jumping when there is a knock at the door or when the telephone rings, or being unable to fall asleep at night due to the sense of vulnerability it brings. Even victims who are no longer being stalked may find that they are easily alarmed.

If you find that you've moved beyond the level of "healthy" fear, there are a few types of self-care that you may wish to consider. Planning and preparing "for the worst" is helpful for many people. This may involve increasing the security around the house, and developing "escape" or "action" plans for you and your loved ones. Don't worry if the measures you take seem irrational or extreme. If you are able to fall asleep at night once you've put a deadbolt on the bedroom door, let the dog in the room, and put a cellular phone on the night-table, that's fine. When you get home, if you need to roam through the house checking under the bed, below the couch cushions, and behind the shower curtain — it's okay, you're not crazy. Many crime survivors develop various daily "habits" to help themselves feel safer. Recognize that personal wellness takes priority over inconvenience to yourself and others. Self-talk plays another important role in reducing fear. Reassure yourself that you've done everything you can right now to feel safe. Tell yourself that you're as prepared as you can possibly be.

I don't know who to trust . . .

I lost my ability to trust. I'm suspicious of everybody now. **Stalking Survivor**

Stalking can drastically change your perceptions of the world around you. Places and people you thought were safe are now questionable. It's perfectly natural for anyone whose trust has been violated to suddenly feel suspicious of everyone. This experience can be especially difficult for those who previously felt that they were able to see the "good" in everyone and tried to treat each new person with respect and dignity. Being forced to alter your beliefs about the people around you is both sad and difficult. It's fairly common for people to swing from one end of the continuum ("most people can be trusted") to the other ("no one can be trusted"). Eventually, many victims are able to strike a balance in the middle, with a heightened sense of awareness and the ability to establish trusting relationships.

> *I used to believe that there was* ***always*** *something good or decent you can find in anyone. This whole experience has unfortunately made me a more skeptical and cynical person. I hate him for that . . .* **Stalking Survivor**

I feel like I don't have any control over my life . . .

When you're being stalked, the sense that you've lost control over your life is greater than can possibly be expressed with words. Every safe space becomes a potential target for the stalker. Your work, school, home, belongings, pets, friends, family, and leisure activities all become vulnerable to the stalker's intrusive behaviors. To make things worse, good intentioned "helpers" often contribute to your loss of control by loading you with unsolicited or unhelpful advice. For some reason, victims of all types of crimes are often perceived as being helpless or weak. It is assumed that you are no longer able to think for yourself and must need others to take over this task for you. Between the stalker and the "rescuers," it can feel like life's rug has been yanked from beneath your feet.

Making your own decisions is the first step towards taking back some sense of control. Remember that you are the expert on your own individual circumstances. From this book, to police, counselors, co-workers, family, and friends you will find options, suggestions, and straight advice. In the end, however, the choices are yours to make. It helps to perceive yourself as the "team leader" of a group of people with whom you are consulting. By weighing the pro's and con's of every decision, you become an active participant in the war against the stalker.

Talking is another way to regain some control over the situation. Stalkers rely on silence and fear. By reaching out for help, you sever one of their most powerful tools — isolation. Some victims have even taken this as far as the media. When the whole community becomes aware of the situation, the stalker's shroud of secrecy is exposed. While this option is certainly not appropriate for all situations, it demonstrates the power of the voice. Whether you decide to talk to your neighbors or the newspaper, the simple act of talking is critical.

> *I wish so much I would have had the courage to talk to someone about what was happening to me. I kept it all inside and it just ate away at my soul. I let him win by staying silent.* **Stalking Survivor**

A final way that some victims find a sense of control is through self-defense or martial arts practice. While it is unlikely that you'll ever use the physical practice of self-defense in a combat situation, the practice alone can have a profound psychological impact. Many victims have said that self-defense courses helped them to *not feel* physically helpless. Though it is not intended to provide you with a false sense of security, it does allow victims to feel more capable, prepared, and in control of their own bodies.

I'm overwhelmed and exhausted — where can I find help?

Approximately one-third of all stalking victims seek some type of mental health counseling (Tjaden and Thoennes 1998). Whether or not you choose to seek professional support, it is important to recognize that stalking can take a significant toll on the psychological well-being of even the very strongest among us. The number one rule regarding self-care is that getting help is *never* a sign of weakness. If anything, it is a sign of strength and self-awareness for both men and women.

Counselors and advocates can come from a wide-variety of professional backgrounds. Psychiatry, psychology, social work, mental health, and family therapy are several common fields of study from which to choose a support person. Most states require some type of licensure of these practitioners. The following are brief descriptions of the skills and backgrounds of professional helpers (note that there is a great degree of overlap across fields of practice):

- ✓ ***Psychiatry:*** Psychiatrists hold medical degrees (M.D.) and are able to prescribe medication. People are frequently referred to psychiatrists for medication to reduce feelings such as depression and anxiety. They typically are not providing therapy to their patients, but are supplementing another therapist's efforts.
- ✓ ***Psychology*:** Psychologists hold doctorate-level degrees (Ed.D., Psy.D., and Ph.D.), and are typically trained to provide therapy and counseling services. They are also qualified to conduct a broad range of psychological tests.
- ✓ ***Social Work:*** Social workers (M.S.W.) can hold a variety of positions. Masters-level clinical (licensed) social workers are able to provide individual and group therapy in most states. Social workers differ from psychologists in that they intervene not only with the individual, but with that person's environment as well. Social workers can function as counselors, advocates, and case managers.
- ✓ ***Mental Health Counseling:*** Mental health counselors (M.H.C.) can also provide therapy and are typically trained to focus on the psychological well-being of a person.
- ✓ ***Marriage and Family Therapy*:** While marriage and family therapists (M.F.T.) provide psychotherapeutic services similar to mental health counselors, social workers, and psychologists, their training emphasizes the functioning of the family system as a whole, and how it impacts the individual.
- ✓ ***Victim Advocacy:*** Victim advocates can come from a variety of professional backgrounds (from social work to criminal justice) and often play a critical role in the crisis and advocacy areas of intervention. While they are not likely to be offering therapy, victim advocates tend to be available for peer support, safety planning, information and referral regarding community services and options, criminal justice support, personal advocacy, and crisis in-

tervention. Because this is a developing field of practice, victim advocates can be both paraprofessionals (trained volunteers) or masters-degreed professionals.

✓ ***Trauma Specialization:*** Any of the above-listed professionals and practitioners may be identified as trauma specialists. After numerous horrible mass disasters in the world, there began a movement to recognize the need for specialized care for persons who've had traumatic experiences. You may wish to seek out a Certified Trauma Specialist (CTS), a registered Traumatologist, or someone who has undergone Critical Incident Stress Debriefing (CISD) training. These individuals should have a heightened sensitivity to the needs of stalking victims.

It's hard to find someone who can really help you. You have to find someone who can understand your problem . . . and you might have to go to several places before you find the right person. **Stalking Survivor**

From whomever you choose to seek assistance, keep in mind that who they are as a person is equally important to their type of credentials. You must be able to feel comfortable and safe with the person who will be helping you. If you have any hesitancy, trust your gut and find someone else. "The most qualified" is not always "the best" when it comes to therapeutic support. Look for qualities such as sensitivity, knowledge of stalking, knowledge of trauma, and willingness to listen and respect your opinions and choices.

I don't know what they did . . . but it worked. They understood and let me talk. Nobody there labeled me.

Stalking Survivor
(Her counselors utilized a specialized treatment technique entitled Traumatic Incident Reduction.)

Ideally, you might want to find both a counselor and a victim advocate to meet all of your psychological and practical needs. When choosing a victim advocate, look for someone who will be able to devote a significant amount of time to your situation. If you are pursuing criminal charges, an advocate will most likely be assigned to your case. In many communities, however, victim advocates can be found at police departments, universities, rape crisis centers, domestic violence centers, crisis hotlines, and other nonprofit organizations.

5

Special Circumstances

As mentioned in the first chapter, stalking occurs across all populations, settings and circumstances. While the information in the previous chapters is intended to help all stalking victims, there are a few circumstances that require additional attention. This chapter will cover the stalking of children, college students, and ex-intimate partners. In each of these situations, there are numerous factors that can aggravate and complicate the problem. These will be discussed, along with further options available under each circumstance.

If Your Child is Being Stalked

Most parents' worst nightmare is the potential loss of or harm to their children. Stalkers pose such threats on a daily basis across the country. Despite the frequency with which this occurs, the stalking of children has received little attention. The State of Florida, however, recently passed a law to make the stalking of children an automatic felony (instead of a misdemeanor). A south Florida parent whose child was stalked helped to push this law through the legislature. Hopefully, the rest of the country won't wait for tragedy to occur before following suit with their own versions of this statute.

Very little is known about the profiles of stalkers who choose children as their targets. Whether they are pedophiles (sexual abusers), sociopaths, or have some other type of mental disorder remains scientifically unknown. Regardless of the source of the problem, stalkers of children can create horrible trauma and terror for entire families. Like adults, children can be stalked by total strangers or trusted acquaintances. They may be adults or other children. In any event, it is important to never underestimate the potential danger of the situation.

If your child is being stalked, you might consider doing the following (in addition to options discussed in Chapter 2):

- ✓ Alert the child's teachers and administrators at his or her school. Describe the stalker and give explicit instructions as to who may pick-up the child from school.
- ✓ If the stalker is another student, push the administration to consider strict punishment, such as expulsion, suspension, and/or transfer to another school. The liability for school districts that are aware of the situation, but have not provided adequate security for victims, is considerable. It is critical, however, for the parents to clearly express their safety concerns to numerous individuals along the "chain of command"(teachers, administrators, school board, superintendent).
- ✓ If possible, arrange for your child to be picked up and dropped off at school by someone you trust.
- ✓ Avoid circumstances where your child might be left alone.
- ✓ Alert neighbors and ask that they contact you (or the police) if they see the stalker.
- ✓ Explore ways to empower your child, such as giving him or her a cellular phone and/or personal alarm, allowing the child to tell the story to the police, and enrolling him or her in martial arts classes.
- ✓ Try to avoid isolating your child. Make sure he or she is able to continue participating in extracurricular activities and spending time with friends under reasonably safe circumstances.

As a final thought, don't forget to attend to your own needs. The experience of parenting alone is cause enough for a fair amount of worrying, without the added trauma of stalking. It is important to get the proper help to allow you and your child adequate sleep, rest, food, and exercise. Occurrences like this put a heavy strain on family and marital relationships. Though safety is a primary concern, be careful not to neglect the emotional well-being of yourself and your family. It may be helpful to seek family therapy during such a stressfull time.

Stalking on College Campuses

Even though stalking is a common occurrence everywhere, college campuses seem to provide a fertile ground for this crime. Though many perceive the campus environment as a "safe haven" away from general community crime, the opposite is often the reality. Between interpersonal and property crimes, college students face a variety of dangers on a daily basis. Campus administrators, law enforcement, and students are just now beginning to recognize stalking as a significant problem. Research has indicated that between one-quarter and one-third of college students have been stalked (Fremouw, et al. 1997; Spitzberg 1998).

Numerous Aspects of Campus Life Allow for Stalking

- The majority of students fall into a "dating" age group and some stalking behaviors seem misconstrued as "normal" dating practices.
- In addition to coursework, many campuses offer entertainment, food service, health care, fitness, recreation, and housing all within a contained community. This allows stalkers frequent opportunities to observe their victims and learn their habits, making it hard for victims to differentiate between "coincidental" appearances and purposeful pursuit.
- A semester is long enough for any stalker to develop an obsession with a classmate.

- Large peer groups offer stalkers the opportunity to find out personal information about their victims in a seemingly harmless manner.
- Since many students stay in the campus environment for four or more years, even "harmless" crushes can evolve over time into serious obsessions.
- For those students who don't work, there are only a few "scheduled" hours out of each day. This leaves a lot of time for stalkers to pursue their victims.
- Students are often asked to provide their social security numbers for a variety of purposes, from obtaining grades to getting inside the fitness center. On some campuses, this may allow stalkers the opportunity to access victims' class schedule and other personal information.

For students being stalked, the ability to focus on their educational goals becomes a huge challenge. It's extremely difficult to concentrate in class if you're worried that your stalker will be waiting outside when you leave, or worse, is sitting inside the classroom with you. Unfortunately, many students find their grades slipping along with their ability to concentrate.

Choices for Students

- Does your college or university have a victim advocate on campus? Sometimes you may find these individuals in women centers, sexual assault offices, student-counseling centers, health clinics, and police departments. If an advocate is available, you might enlist his or her assistance to help you contact other campus resources.
- Can your student identification number be changed?
- Can you change your class schedule by switching sections of the same course? Sometimes professors allow their students to transfer over to another colleague's classroom.
- If you are nearing the end of the semester, would it be possible to complete some coursework at home?

- Would it be helpful to take an incomplete in any of your classes?
- Have you considered telling your instructors what is happening and requesting their assistance (or support to change the parameters of your coursework)?
- If the stalker is another student, is it possible to pursue help through your campus' judicial system?
- Would you like to report the problem to the campus police department?
- If you feel you must quit school and relocate, have you thought about transferring to another school? Sometimes under these circumstances, all course credits can be accepted by another institution.

As more and more victims of stalking on campus come forward, colleges and universities will become more prepared to handle these situations. Many schools have incorporated anti-stalking guidelines into their codes of conduct and established support services for victims. If these are not available at your institution, you may find that you are forced to be a vocal advocate for yourself. Under these circumstances, you might find the support of community victim advocates, police departments and prosecutor offices to be quite helpful.

When the Relationship is Over: Stalking of Ex-Intimate Partners

> *You have to decide that you don't want to see this person anymore. You have to decide that you've had enough, that it's over . . . Whatever you do, don't let him [or her] decide for you.* **Stalking Survivor**

Some of the most complex cases of stalking involve people who have previously held romantic relationships. Since stalkers rely on victims' personal information to terrorize them, ex-partners are at an obvious disadvantage. To make matters worse, these stalkers tend to be the most likely to use physical violence against their victims. While domestic violence has received a great deal of national attention in the past several years, the end of these relationships often triggers a new nightmare involving stalking. In some cases, the stalking is so awful that victims return to their partners in an attempt to survive and protect their family. Others decide to flee across the state or country and change their identities — giving up careers, friendships, homes and close proximity to family members.

Since ex-intimate stalking often escalates to serious levels, it is important for victims to engage in risk assessment and safety planning. If threats like "If I can't have you, nobody will" have been made, or there was physical abuse during the relationship, recognize that you are in danger. Many victims believe they will be able to "talk" the stalker out of harming them, or think that the stalker wouldn't ever really hurt them. Unfortunately, once you realize they can and will hurt you, it is too late. Stalkers' desperation can lead them to do things you'd never believe they were even capable of.

> *I had to realize this person was broken and there was nothing I could do to put him back together — nothing I could do to fix him.* **Stalking Survivor**

If you believe you might be at risk for physical harm, there are a variety of options you might want to consider:

- ✓ Tell everyone who knows you and your ex-partner that he or she is stalking you. This will help prevent people from unwittingly telling the stalker where you are or what you're doing.
- ✓ Notify the police departments where you live and work that you are in danger. They may suggest you get a restraining order so they can arrest the stalker if he or she contacts you.
- ✓ If you have children, arrange visitation through a third party. Do not meet the stalker, even if it is in a public place, to drop off and pick up the children.

- ✓ If you have left your home or apartment and must return to pick up your belongings, do so only with a police escort. Do not bring a friend and assume you will be safe.
- ✓ If you live in a guarded community, give the security manager a photo (or physical description) of the stalker and tell them to call the police if he or she tries to enter the area.
- ✓ Develop safety plans for yourself, your children, and local friends and family. The stalker may try to use any leverage he or she has against you, which could involve threats to your loved ones.
- ✓ If you decide to start dating someone new — this person is at risk for harm. Stalking behaviors often escalate when the stalker perceives a new threat. Make sure that anyone you become involved with is fully aware of the situation.
- ✓ If you must flee for your safety, consider seeking help at domestic violence shelters. If you are a male and not permitted to stay at a shelter for women, ask if they have funds to pay for a hotel room. If the stalker knows the location of the shelter, their staff can assist you in locating another shelter in a different region.
- ✓ Learn what laws and services exist in your community to protect you. Some areas have developed elaborate systems to combat domestic violence. You may be eligible for a free cellular phone or other forms of added protection.

Finally, victims of ex-partner stalking must also recognize they've been doubly traumatized. Being betrayed by a person whom you loved and trusted adds to the horror of being hunted. Consider seeking professional help to work through the layers of pain, abuse, and deception. Also, it may be helpful to find a counselor who specializes in domestic violence. Even the most sensitive professional can do more harm than good if he or she has not had specific training in this area.

Remember:

It doesn't matter whether you love them, hate them, give them compassion or give them anger . . . they'll take any emotion you have to offer. Whatever you have, they'll take it. All they really want is a reaction — good or bad. There's nothing you can do to please them.

Stalking Survivor

Appendix A
Sample Stalking Journal

Date and Time	Location	Description	Response	Witnesses
9/30/98 @ 9:50 p.m.	Home	J. Doe left a message on my answering machine stating "If you don't talk to me, you'll regret it."	Removed cassette tape and saved it in a dated envelope.	None
10/4/98 @ 11:00 a.m.	Work	Through my window, I observed J. Doe drive by our office 16 times between 11 a.m. and 1 p.m.	Called the company's security guard, who documented the last six times.	Ana Smith Carl Joseph Melinda Garcia
10/5/98 @ 5:30 p.m.	Parking lot of workplace	As I was walking to my car, J. Doe approached me and demanded that I stop to talk.	I continued to walk towards my car, but J. grabbed my arm and yanked me back. I broke free and ran back into the building and called security.	None — when security arrived, J. had already left the premises.

Date and Time	Location	Description	Response	Witnesses
10/5/98 @ 10:00 p.m.	Home	J. Doe came to my house and started banging and kicking the door, demanding to be let inside.	I called 911 and waited five minutes until the police came. J. started to run away when they pulled onto my street, but Officer Johns was able to catch J. A report was filed at the Jackson City P.D. under # 9807654.	Officer Johns Officer Brown Marianna Dole (neighbor at 1121 W. 4th St.)
10/12/98 @ 7:30 a.m.	Home	When I unlocked my car door this morning, I discovered that blue ink had been spilled on the driver's seat. It left a stain approximately five inches long and two inches wide.	I called the Jackson City police department. They filed an incident report under # 9808976. I requested that they file the incident report together with the other report from 10/5/98.	Officer Marham took a polariod photo and a sample of the ink stain.

Appendix B
Building a Prosecutable Case Checklist

- ✓ ❑ Keep a detailed log.
- ✓ ❑ Obtain a copy of your state's stalking law.
- ✓ ❑ Keep a file of all police reports.
- ✓ ❑ Make sure each police department (for multiple jurisdictions) has copies of each other's reports.
- ✓ ❑ Make sure each new police report makes reference to prior reports.
- ✓ ❑ Maintain regular contact with detectives assigned to your case.
- ✓ ❑ Obtain assistance from a victim advocate.
- ✓ ❑ Report every incident (especially violations of restraining orders).
- ✓ ❑ Keep all evidence.
- ✓ ❑ Save all forms of Internet (e-mail) communications.
- ✓ ❑ Report e-mail harassment to your Internet provider (such as AOL or Prodigy).
- ✓ ❑ Save phone messages on removable answering machine cassettes.
- ✓ ❑ Use call trace (typically *57) immediately after a harassing telephone call and notify police that you have traced the call.

- ✓ ❑ Ask friends, neighbors, co-workers, and family to write down any communications or contact (including observation) they have had with the stalker.
- ✓ ❑ If possible rent a surveillance camera to capture the stalker on video.
- ✓ ❑ Consider obtaining a restraining order to bolster the strength of the legal case.

Appendix C
Safety Checklist

Home

- ✓ ❑ Add alarm system (or small motion-sensor alarms) to home or apartment.
- ✓ ❑ Trim bushes and trees around home to eliminate or reduce hiding places.
- ✓ ❑ Place security pins in windows and sliding glass doors.
- ✓ ❑ Install bars across the center of sliding glass doors.
- ✓ ❑ Make sure deadbolts are secured with screws at least two inches long.
- ✓ ❑ Attach motion-sensor lights to outside of home.
- ✓ ❑ Install locks on bedroom doors.
- ✓ ❑ Install panoramic peepholes on entry doors.
- ✓ ❑ Keep a cellular phone inside the home (in case phone lines are cut).
- ✓ ❑ Keep important documents in a security box at a bank.
- ✓ ❑ Keep an "escape" bag (with necessary daily items) at the home of a trusted friend.
- ✓ ❑ Consider getting a dog.

Car

- ✓ ❑ Peer inside and underneath car before entering.
- ✓ ❑ Vary the routes you take to places of frequent travel.
- ✓ ❑ Drive with your doors locked at all times.
- ✓ ❑ Always leave enough space between you and the car in front of you to quickly change lanes.
- ✓ ❑ Consult with a locksmith about enhancing the locking mechanisms on your vehicle.
- ✓ ❑ If the stalker somehow gets inside the car with you, avoid driving anywhere. If possible, throw the keys as far away as you can.

Work

- ✓ ❑ Make sure all of your co-workers are aware of the stalking.
- ✓ ❑ If possible, vary your work schedule.
- ✓ ❑ Have someone else record your voicemail message, so that it is not your own voice.
- ✓ ❑ Seek escorts to and from your car.
- ✓ ❑ If possible, eliminate times you are working by yourself.
- ✓ ❑ Instruct all persons at your work place to refuse to disclose any information about you to a third party.
- ✓ ❑ Ask your co-workers to not communicate with the stalker.

Public

✓ ❑ Vary your daily routine.

✓ ❑ Tell only trusted individuals about your future plans.

✓ ❑ If you have a restraining order, carry it with you at all times.

✓ ❑ Tell companions that you are being stalked.

✓ ❑ Avoid isolated places such as alleyways, restrooms, etc.

Notify Sources of Information of the Need for Privacy

✓ ❑ Phone company

✓ ❑ Utilities (electric, water, sewer)

✓ ❑ Homeowner Association

✓ ❑ City Hall

✓ ❑ Post Office (consider getting a P.O. Box for your mailing address)

✓ ❑ Newspaper delivery

✓ ❑ Internet provider

✓ ❑ Employer

✓ ❑ Professional associations

✓ ❑ Club memberships (fitness, hobbies, music, books, wine, discount stores, sports, etc.)

✓ ❑ Pizza delivery

✓ ❑ Church

- ✓ ❑ Schools where you are currently or have been previously enrolled
- ✓ ❑ School reunion committees (high school and college)
- ✓ ❑ Video rental stores
- ✓ ❑ Doctors' offices
- ✓ ❑ Pharmacy
- ✓ ❑ Insurance agencies
- ✓ ❑ Landlord or rental agencies
- ✓ ❑ Magazine subscriptions
- ✓ ❑ Credit card companies
- ✓ ❑ Charities
- ✓ ❑ Blood drive committees
- ✓ ❑ Social security office
- ✓ ❑ Drivers license office
- ✓ ❑ Tax collector
- ✓ ❑ Other? ______________________________

Appendix D: U. S. Interstate Domestic Violence and Stalking Laws

(Amended September, 1996)

SOURCE:
UNITED STATES CODE
TITLE 18 — CRIMES AND CRIMINAL PROCEDURE
PART I — CRIMES
CHAPTER 110A — DOMESTIC VIOLENCE AND STALKING

Sec. 2261. Interstate domestic violence

(a) Offenses. —

(1) Crossing a state line. — A person who travels across a State line or enters or leaves Indian country with the intent to injure, harass, or intimidate that person's spouse or intimate partner, and who, in the course of or as a result of such travel, intentionally commits a crime of violence and thereby causes bodily injury to such spouse or intimate partner, shall be punished as provided in subsection (b).

(2) Causing the crossing of a state line. — A person who causes a spouse or intimate partner to cross a State line or to enter or leave Indian country by force, coercion, duress, or fraud, and, in the course or as a result of that conduct, intentionally commits a crime of violence and thereby causes bodily injury to the person's spouse or intimate partner, shall be punished as provided in subsection (b).

(b) Penalties. — A person who violates this section or section 2261A shall be fined under this title, imprisoned —

(1) for life or any term of years, if death of the victim results;

(2) for not more than 20 years if permanent disfigurement or life-threatening bodily injury to the victim results;

(3) for not more than 10 years, if serious bodily injury to the victim results or if the offender uses a dangerous weapon during the offense;

(4) as provided for the applicable conduct under chapter 109A if the offense would constitute an offense under chapter 109A (without regard to whether the offense was committed in the special maritime and territorial jurisdiction of the United States or in a Federal prison); and

(5) for not more than 5 years, in any other case, or both fined and imprisoned.

Sec. 2261A. Interstate stalking

Whoever travels across a State line or within the special maritime and territorial jurisdiction of the United States with the intent to injure or harass another person, and in the course of, or as a result of, such travel places that person in reasonable fear of the death of, or serious bodily injury (as defined in section 1365(g)(3) of this title) to, that person or a member of that person's immediate family (as defined in section 115 of this title) shall be punished as provided in section 2261 of this title.

§ 2262. Interstate violation of protection order

(a) Offenses. —

(1) Crossing a state line. — A person who travels across a State line or enters or leaves Indian country with the intent to engage in conduct that —

(A)(i) violates the portion of a protection order that involves protection against credible threats of violence, repeated harassment, or bodily injury to the person or persons for whom the protection order was issued; or

(ii) would violate subparagraph (A) if the conduct occurred in the jurisdiction in which the order was issued;

and (B) subsequently engages in such conduct, shall be punished as provided in subsection (b).

(2) Causing the crossing of a state line. — A person who causes a spouse or intimate partner to cross a State line or to enter or leave Indian country by force, coercion, duress, or fraud, and, in the course or as a result of that conduct, intentionally commits an act that injures the person's spouse or intimate partner in violation of a valid protection order issued by a State shall be punished as provided in subsection (b).

(b) Penalties. — A person who violates this section shall be fined under this title, imprisoned —

(1) for life or any term of years, if death of the offender's spouse or intimate partner results;

(2) for not more than 20 years if permanent disfigurement or life-threatening bodily injury to the offender's spouse or intimate partner results;

(3) for not more than 10 years, if serious bodily injury to the offender's spouse or intimate partner results or if the offender uses a dangerous weapon during the offense;

(4) as provided for the applicable conduct under chapter 109A if the offense would constitute an offense under chapter 109A (without regard to whether the offense was committed in the special maritime and territorial jurisdiction of the United States or in a Federal prison); and

(5) for not more than 5 years, in any other case, or both fined and imprisoned.

Appendix E
National Hotlines and Sources of Information

☎ National Victim Center (NVC)
1-800-FYI-CALL (394-2255)

☎ National Organization of Victim Assistance (NOVA)
24 Hour Line 1-800-TRY NOVA (879-6682)

☎ Office for Victims of Crime Resource Center
1-800-627-6872

☎ Workplace Violence Resource Center
704-720-0854

☎ National Center for Women and Family Law
212-674-8200

☎ National Clearinghouse for the Defense of Battered Women
215-351-0010

☎ National Criminal Justice Reference Service
1-800-851-34200

☎ National Resource Center on Domestic Violence
1-800-537-2238

☎ Resource Center on Child Protection and Custody
1-800-527-3223

☎ Rape, Abuse, and Incest National Network (RAIN)
1-800-656-4673

☎ National Domestic Violence Hotline
1-800-799-7233

☎ National Center for Missing and Exploited Children
1-800-843-5678

World Wide Web Sites

- Survivors of Stalking
  http://www.soshelp.org
- Stalking Victims Sanctuary
  http://www.stalkingvictims.com
- The Anti-Stalking Website
  http://www.antistalking.com
- Victim Assistance On-Line
  http://www.vaonline.org
- National Victim Center (maintains a list of U.S. state stalking laws)
  http://www.nvc.org/
- Florida International Victim Advocacy Center
  http://www.fiu.edu/~victimad
- Privacy Rights Clearinghouse
  http://www.privacyrights.org
- Office for Victims of Crime (U.S. Dept. of Justice, Office of Justice Programs)
  http://www.ojp.usdoj.gov/ovc/
- Results from national stalking study (Department of Justice)
  http://www.ncjrs.org/txtfiles/fs000186.txt
- NOVA (National Organization of Victim Assistance)
  http://www.trynova.org
- Sexual Assault Information Pages
  http://www.cs.utk.edu/%7Ebartley/saInfoPage.html
- David Baldwin's Trauma Pages
  http://www.trauma-pages.com
- National Center for Post Traumatic Stress Disorder Information
  http://www.dartmouth.edu/dms/ptsd
- International Society for Traumatic Stress Studies
  http://www.istss.com

- International Critical Incident Stress Foundation
  http://www.icisf.org
- FIND LAW (Internet Resource About Legal Issues)
  http://findlaw.com

Appendix F
Related Readings

De Becker, G. *The Gift of Fear: Survival Skills that Protect us from Violence.* New York: Little Brown and Company, 1997.

Gross, L. *To Have or to Harm.* New York: Warner Books, 1994.

Orion, D. *I know You Really Love Me.* New York: Dell Publishing, 1998.

Schaum, M., and K. Parrish. *Stalked.* New York: Pocket Books, 1995.

Scott, M. *How to Lose Anyone Anywhere.* Kalamazoo: Stealth Publishing, 1998.

Appendix G
Selected Bibliography

Anderson, S. C. "Anti-Stalking Laws: Will They Curb the Erotomanic's Obsessive Pursuit?" *Law and Psychology Review* 17 (1993): 171-91.

Coleman, F. L. "Stalking Behavior and the Cycle of Domestic Violence." *Journal of Interpersonal Violence* 12/3 (1997): 420-32.

Fein, R. A., B. Vossekuil, and G. Holden. *Threat Assessment: An Approach to Prevent Targeted Violence.* National Institute of Justice: Research in Action, July 1-7, 1995.

Fremouw, W. J., D. Westrup, and J. Pennypacker. "Stalking on Campus: The Prevalence and Strategies for Coping with Stalking." *Journal of Forensic Science* 42/4 (1997): 666-69.

Fritz, J. P. "A Proposal for Mental Health Provisions in State Anti-stalking Laws." *The Journal of Psychiatry and Law* (Summer 1995): 295-318.

Hall, D. M. "Outside Looking In: Stalkers and their Victims." *Dissertation Abstracts International* 58-08A (1997): 3314.

Harmon, R. B., R. Rosner, and H. Owens. "Obsessional Harassment and Erotomania in a Criminal Court Population" *Journal of Forensic Sciences* 40/20 (1995): 188-96.

Meloy, J. R. "Unrequited Love and the Wish to Kill: Diagnosis and Treatment of Borderline Erotomania." *Bulletin of the Menninger Clinic* 53 (1989): 477-92.

Meloy, J. R. "Stalking (Obsessional Following): A Review of Some Preliminary Studies." *Aggression and Violent Behavior* 1/2 (1996): 147-62.

Meloy, J. R. (ed.). *The Psychology of Stalking: Clinical and Forensic Perspectives.* San Diego: Academic Press, 1998.

Meloy, J. R. "The Clinical Risk Management of Stalking: "Someone is Watching Over Me . . ." *American Journal of Psychotherapy* 51/2 (1997): 174-84.

Mullen, P. E., and E. Pathe'. "The Pathological Extensions of Love." *British Journal of Psychiatry* 165 (1994): 614-23.

Mullen, P. E., and E. Pathe'. "Stalking and the Pathologies of Love." *Australian and New Zealand Journal of Psychiatry* 28 (1994): 469-77.

National Criminal Justice Association. *Project to Develop a Model Anti-Stalking Code for States.* Washington, D.C.: U.S. National Institute of Justice, 1993.

Pathe', E., and P. E. Mullen." The Impact of Stalkers on Their Victims." *The British Journal of Psychiatry* 170 (1997): 12-17.

Roberts, A. R., and S. F. Dziegielewski. "Assessment Typology and Intervention with the Survivors of Stalking." *Aggression and Violent Behavior* 1/4 (1996): 359-68.

Romans, S. C., J. R. Hays, and T. K. White. "Stalking and Related Behaviors Experienced by Counseling Center Staff Members From Current or Former Clients." *Professional Psychology: Research and Practice* 27/6 (1996): 595-99.

Spitzberg, B., A. Nicastro, and A. Cousins. "Exploring the Interactional Phenomenon of Stalking and Obsessive Relational Intrusion." *Communication Reports* 11/1 (1998): 33-47.

Tjaden, P., and N. Thoenes. "Stalking in America: Findings from the National Violence Against Women Survey." *National Institute of Justice Centers for Disease Control and Prevention Research in Brief* (April 1998).

United States Senate, Committee on the Judiciary. *Anti-Stalking Proposals: First Session on Combating Stalking and Family Violence.* Serial no. J-103-5. Washington D.C.: U.S. Government Printing Office, 1993.

United States Senate, Committee on the Judiciary. *Combating Violence Against Women: Second Session on S. 1729, a Bill to*

Amend Title 18, United States Code, with Respect to Stalking. Serial no. J-104-81. Washington, D.C.: U.S., Government Printing Office, 1996.

Williams, W. L., J. Lane, and M. A Zona. "Stalking: Successful Intervention Strategies." *The Police Chief* 2 (1996): 24-26.

Wright, J. A., A. G. Burgess, A. W. Burgess, A. T. Lazlo, G. O. McCrary, and J. E. Douglas. "A Typology of Interpersonal Stalking." *Journal of Interpersonal Violence* 11/4 (1996): 487-502.

Zona, M. A., K. K. Sharma, and J. Lane. "A Comparative Study of Erotomanic and Obsessional Subjects in a Forensic Sample." *Journal of Forensic Sciences* 38/4 (1993): 894-903.